Soldiering On

A monologue from *Talking Heads*

Alan Bennett

GW00455283

Samuel French—London
New York-Toronto-Hollywood

ISBN 0 573 13311 5

Please see page iv for further copyright information

SOLDIERING ON

First shown on BBC TV on 10th May 1988. The cast was as follows:

Muriel   Stephanie Cole

Directed by Tristram Powell
Produced by Innes Lloyd
Designed by Tony Burrough

Subsequently performed as part of the stage version of *Talking Heads*, produced by Duncan Weldon Management, which opened on February 8th 1993 at the Theatre Royal, Newcastle. The cast was as follows:

Muriel   Gwen Watford

Directed by Alan Bennett
Designed by Simon Higlett
Lighting by Paul Pyant

SOLDIERING ON

At the back of the stage is a flat, papered in a vaguely up-market wallpaper, maybe with a pelmet or picture-rail. There is an upright upholstered armchair DR *and an upright chair* UL *with a side table to its* R

Muriel is a brisk, sensible woman in her fifties. She is in a tweed skirt and cardigan with a single row of pearls. She stands downstage, C

Muriel It's a funny time, three o'clock, too late for lunch but a bit early for tea. Besides, there were one or two brave souls who'd trekked all the way from Wolverhampton; I couldn't risk giving them tea or we'd have had a mutiny on our hands. And I think people like to be offered something even if they don't actually eat it. One's first instinct was to make a beeline for the freezer and rout out the inevitable quiche, but I thought, 'Muriel, old girl, that's the coward's way out,' so the upshot was I stopped up till two in the morning trundling out a selection of my old standards ... chicken in a lemon sauce, beef *en croute* from the old Colchester days (I thought of Jessie Marchant), and bushels of assorted salads. As it happened it wasn't exactly a salady day, quite crisp for April actually, however Mabel warmed up the proceedings with one of her famous soups, conjured up out of thin air, so we lived to fight another day. Nobody could quite put their finger on the flavour, so I was able to go around saying, 'Have you guessed the soup yet?' and that broke the ice a bit. I don't know what got into Mabel but she'd gone mad and added a pinch of curry and that foxed most people.

She sits in the armchair

It was cauliflower actually.

Still, it was a bit sticky at the start as these occasions generally are. There were people there one didn't know from Adam (all the Massey-Ferguson people for instance, completely unknown quantities to me), and then lots of people I knew I should know and didn't. But whenever I saw someone looking lost I thought of Ralph and grabbed hold of someone I did know and breezed up saying, 'This is Jocelyn. She's at the Royal College of Art. I don't know your name but the odds are you're in agricultural machinery,' and then left them to it. It was a case of light the blue touch paper and retire.

Knowing Ralph, of course, it was a real mixed bag. Several there from the Sports Council and quite a contingent from Tonbridge, some Friends of Norwich Cathedral and the Discharged Prisoners Aid Society, Madge and Perce whom we met on the *Mauretania* on our honeymoon, Donald and Joyce Bannerman who were actually *en route* for Abu Dhabi, then Donald bought a paper at Heathrow, saw the announcement and came straight down. And one sweet old man who'd come all the way over from Margate. He said, 'You won't remember me, Mrs Carpenter, but I'm a member of the criminal fraternity.' I shrieked. As the vicar said: Ralph touched life at many points.

The children magnificent, of course, or Giles at any rate. Luckily Margaret didn't appear. But Giles took off all the Household Brigade people on a tour of the garden while Pippa coped with some of the bigwigs from the City. 'I don't think you know George,' I heard one of them say, 'George cracks the whip at Goodison, Brown.' Poor souls, they both of them deserved medals. And Crispin and Lucy angelic, Crispin popping in and out of people's legs reaching up to fill glasses. I wanted them to have a rest. 'No,' said Giles, 'let them do it. They adored their Grandpa.' 'Adored him,' said Pippa, 'like we all did.'

The church had been absolutely chocker and I managed not to blub until right at the finish when they struck up with 'I Vow To Thee My Country.' And then I had a hundred and one things to do so I was perfectly all right until I saw Angela Gillespie had made the mistake of talking to boring old Frank from the firm, and I heard the dreaded words 'fork-lift trucks' and thought how many times I used to have to shut Ralph up in similar circumstances, and the idea of shutting Ralph up at all set me off instantly and I had to nip into the pantry to staunch the flow, shortly to be followed by Mabel who'd just fallen over one of his old wellingtons and promptly gone into floods. So we had a good laugh and a good cry over that before powdering our noses and hurling ourselves back into the fray.

When everybody'd gone I'm just having five minutes in the chair before tackling the debris when Margaret comes plunging into the room. She said, 'What were all those people?' I said, 'It was a kind of party for Daddy.' She said 'Why ? Is he dead?' I said 'You know he's dead.' She said, 'Who killed him?' I said 'Don't be such a donkey. Come along and we'll find you a tablet.' Some of Ralph's medicine's still in the cupboard. Fat lot of good that did, I thought, and poured it down the lav. Then felt a bit choked.

Anyway the tablet did the trick. I heard her walking about at two in the morning but I didn't get up. Except then I had to get up anyway because it suddenly came to me, in all the excitement I'd completely forgotten to feed the dogs.

She exits UL

Music; the Lights fade to Black-out

Muriel enters R *and sits in the armchair*

The Lights come up; the music fades

Everybody I run into says not to take any big decisions. I staggered into the Community Centre bearing Ralph's entire wardrobe which Angela Gillespie had nipped in smartish and earmarked for Muscular Dystrophy. Five minutes later, Brenda Bousfield had come knocking at the door on behalf of Cystic Fibrosis. Knives out straightaway, I practically had to separate them. In fact I did separate

them in the end, the city suits to Angela and Brenda the tweeds. All
lovely stuff. Beautiful dinner jacket from Hawes and Curtis, done
for Giles if he hadn't got so fat. Mind you, he didn't want the ties
either. Angela did. 'Lovely jumble,' she said. 'How're you coping?
Don't take any big decisions, one day at a time, I don't see any
shoes.'

Actually I'd been silly and kept his shoes back. I loved his shoes.
Always used to clean them. 'My shoeshine lady.' 'Whatever you
do,' Angela said, 'don't give them to Brenda. They're top-heavy on
staff, their group, it's well known. It all goes on the admin. We can
use shoes.'

She moves to the chair UL *and sits*

I thought I'd go into the library and see if Miss Dunsmore could find
me something on bereavement. That's something I learned from
Ralph: plug into other people's experience, pool your resources. 'A
new experience is like travelling through unknown country. But
remember, others have taken this road before you, old girl, and left
notes. So Question no. 1: Is there a map? Question no. 2: Am I taking
advantage of all the information available? It doesn't matter if
you're going to get married, commit a burglary or keep a guinea pig;
efficiency is the proper collation of information.' Oh Ralph.

Miss Dunsmore did a reconnoitre round, but the only information
she could come up with was a book about burial customs in Papua,
New Guinea. I think even Ralph would draw the line at that.
However, she thought the Health Centre did a pamphlet on bereavement. Miss Dunsmore said she wasn't offering this as consolation
but apparently elephants go into mourning and so, very strangely,
does the pike. So we chatted about that for a bit. Told me not to take
any big decisions, and if I was throwing away any of his books could
I steer them her way as she ran some sort of reading service for the
disabled.

She returns to the armchair and sits

I dropped into the Health Centre and the receptionist said there was a pamphlet on death; they'd had some on the counter, only the tots kept taking them to scribble on, so they hadn't re-ordered. She said she'd skimmed through it and the gist of it was not to take any big decisions and to throw yourself into something. I said, 'You don't mean the canal?' She said, 'Come again?' Nobody expects you to make jokes. As I was going out she called me back and said did Ralph wear spectacles? Because if he did, not to throw away the old pairs as owing to cutbacks they'd started a spectacles recycling scheme.

Back at base Mabel said Margaret had been plonked on the chair in the passage all morning with her bag packed and her outside coat on, and for some reason wellington boots. Said the police were coming. We manhandled her upstairs, and after about seventeen goes I managed to smuggle in a tablet which did the trick and she'd just settled down for a little zizz when who should draw up at the door but Giles.

She rises and moves DL

He'd cancelled all his appointments, eluded the guards at the office and just belted down the A12 because he suddenly thought I might need cheering up, bless him. He could always get round Mabel ever since he was little, so she agrees to hold the fort while he whisks me off to lunch at somewhere rather swish. I thought to myself, I hope you're watching, Ralph, you old rascal, and eating your words. Ralph and Giles never got on for more than five minutes whereas, it's funny, he was always dotty about Mags.

When eventually we get back, what with all the wine et cetera (I mean pudding *and* cheese), I'm just longing to put my head down ——

She moves C

—— but Giles cracks the whip and gets me to sign lots of papers. It turns out Ralph's left me very nicely off. What with the house and all the various holdings, one way or another I'm quite a rich lady. He's tied a bit up for Margaret, nothing specific for Giles, but he doesn't mind because of course he doesn't need any and when I go he'll get it anyway. But what I do have is what Giles calls a liquidity problem, and the first item on the agenda is to give me some ready cash, hence the papers. Then something about buying a forest. Bit wary to start with, said, 'Can I not mull it?' and Giles said, 'Well you can, but the index is going down.' I said, 'What about Mr Sherlock?' Giles said, 'You know what lawyers are.' Wish old Ralph could have seen me, signing away. He never showed me any papers at all. I suppose it's a different generation.

She moves to the armchair and sits

What he did do, which made me feel a tiny bit shifty, was to take away three or four of the best pictures, the two carriage clocks and a couple of other choice items. Said that when the sharks from the revenue came round to assess the stuff for estate duty these were just the items that would bump the figure up. I said, 'What about the inventory?' Giles said, 'I think we'll just drag our brogues on that one.' Apparently everybody does it. He's just going to keep the stuff under the bed at Sloane Street until the heat is off, then back they come.

Margaret still lying on the bed when I went upstairs. Asleep she looks quite presentable. Daddy's little girl. Not so little now, those great legs. But as Mabel says, 'It looks as if we're on the hospital trail again.' If she goes in, I could perhaps go to Siena. Except I've nobody to go with. One keeps forgetting that.

Music. The Lights fade to Black-out

 Muriel exits UL *behind the flat, then enters* R *with some envelopes which she puts on the side table. She then sits in the armchair*

The Lights come up; the music fades

It's not an ideal place, no -one is saying it is. Even Giles doesn't say that. In fact it's a perfect example of one of those places they're always famously about to scrap. Started life as a workhouse probably, during the Napoleonic Wars, and *qua* building not displeasing. As someone weaned on Nikolaus Pevsner and practically a founding member of the National Trust I wouldn't alter a single brick. And as an arts centre first rate. As a museum of industrial archaeology ... couldn't be bettered. Or as a craft centre, weaving, pottery, a shop-window where craftsmen and craftswomen could make and display their wares ... absolutely ideal, the very place. But as a mental hospital ... oh no, no, no, no, no.

The food, for instance. The food has to cross a courtyard — the kitchen is so far away for all I know it may have to cross a frontier. One toilet per floor ... I just put my head round the door and wished I hadn't; no telephone that I could see and the beds so crammed together if you got out of one you'd be into another. Dreadful.

And of course I keep thinking of Ridgeways, the cup of tea, the matron's parlour and that immaculate lawn. It would break old Ralph's heart. But Ridgeways costs money. It always did. First of the month, beg to inform, respectfully submit, all very nice but six hundred pounds on the dot. And more. And more. And as Giles says, 'Mummy no can do. That kind of money we do not have.' Well we do, but it's all tied up.

And whereas in normal circumstances one would have fought tooth and nail to keep her in the private sector, just out of respect for Daddy, nowadays we are in what Giles calls a different ball game. And the old thing minds. Goodness, he minds. I wanted him to come with me today but just the idea of the place upsets him so much he won't even set foot in it. And actually I feel the same, but where is that going to get us? I thought of Ralph (as if I ever think of anybody else) and I thought, 'Come on, Muriel. You're a widow lady, you've got time on your hands, if anybody's in a position to roll their sleeves up it's you.' So today ——

She moves DC

— when I paid Mags a visit I got the name of the hospital secretary,
almoner it used to be called in my day, and bearded him in his den.
He did have a beard actually and looked pretty sorry for himself
besides. It turns out he has to precept for absolutely everything down
to the last toilet roll, and if he does have any brainwaves about
improvements and can sell them to his own management commit-
tee, he's still at the mercy of the regional spending programme.

I asked about a table-tennis table. He said, 'My point exactly.' A
table-tennis table would mean going cap in hand to Ipswich, which
he's not anxious to do since the vegetable steamer's on its last legs.
And on the rare occasions he does have a bit of latitude he finds his
hands are tied by NUPE.

She picks up the letters and sits in the armchair

Well, the upshot is I'm writing sheaves of letters to everybody I've
ever heard of in an effort to plug the hospital into the coffee-morning
circuit and get a support group started. What I'm saying is that
mental illness is a scourge. It's also a mystery, can occur in the best-
regulated families and nobody knows why. I mean, take us. Why
have we been singled out? Loving parents. Perfectly normal child-
hood, then this.

When I went in this afternoon, Margaret was weaving a basket, and
not making a bad stab at it really, all things considered. It's lucky I
arrived when I did because she'd just got to the part where she had
to integrate the handle with the main body and she was making a real
pig's breakfast of it. So I got cracking and showed her the whys and
wherefores and actually ended up making both handles. Which
seemed to make her a lot happier. She's never been much good with
her hands. Giles was a real wizard.

A propos Giles there's a bit of a crisis with the funds apparently.
Nothing serious. A chum's let him down. Didn't read the small

print. Says it's nothing to worry about, though we may have to pull
our horns in a bit further. So I said, 'All hands to the pumps. With
all Daddy's contacts in the City why don't I start up a little catering
business, executive lunches and the like? Good nursery food and
lashings of it.' Giles not sure. Thought these days they wanted
somehing a bit more *nouvelle*. I laughed, I said, 'Don't you believe
it. Men are overgrown schoolboys, always were. Preached salad at
Ralph for years and what good did it do?' Giles said, 'Small detail,
Mum: what are you going to use for capital?' So that put the tin hat
on that one. It's this bloody liquidity thing. It's funny I never heard
Ralph mention it.

Music. The Lights fade to Black-out

> *Muriel picks up the side table and moves it close to the flat, then
> takes the upright chair off stage. She enters L with a tea chest, puts
> it down and stands behind the armchair*

The Lights come up; the music fades

Job sorting out one or two things I want to keep, though quite
honestly I'm not sorry to see the back of most of it. I feel it puts me
more in the same boat as Ralph. Lay not up for yourself treasures on
earth type thing. The lilies of the field syndrome.

She moves DL

Said this to the vicar who was looking round. He thought this was
a healthy attitude and how much did I think the walnut side table
might fetch, it would go well in their hall. Huge marquee on the
lawn. People trooping through the house, and Angela Gillespie
never away. Said how horrid it must be to see people poking about
among one's prized possessions. I said, 'Yes,' but it isn't really. The
person I do feel sorry for is Mabel, who's had it to polish all these
years. Still, she was getting on like a house on fire with the
auctioneer's men, who were all so careful and polite. I'd have
married any one of them on the spot. Angela beefing on about all the

dealers being here, putting up the prices, I thought good job. Still, however much it all fetches it will only be a drop in the ocean.

At one point Angela got the Duttons in a corner and started telling the tale. Said Giles had always been a wrong 'un. I turned round and said she didn't know what she was talking about, it had been a genuine mistake. She said, 'Mistake? Hundreds of people losing their life savings a mistake?' I said, 'So why do you think I'm selling up?' She said, 'It wasn't your fault. Why should you suffer? That's what worries me, Muriel, it's not fair on you.' Fair on me or not it didn't stop her buying the corner cupboard. She's had her eye on it for years.

I suppose Giles has been a scamp, but I don't think he's been wicked. Just not very bright that's all. Still, Sloane Street is in Pippa's name so that's a blessing, and the school fees were covenanted for years ago. So it's not all gloom. And I'm hanging on to this chair. One of the men was putting a label on it; I said 'No fear. This is the one chair in the house that does for the old back.' I sat under the chestnut tree while the sale was going on, and thought how none of this would have happened if Ralph hadn't died. Then I heard him say, 'Buck up, old girl,' and went and gave a hand with the tea. I haven't told Margaret yet. Her fourteen-year-old psychiatrist thinks this may not be the moment. Sees some signs of improvement. Margaret brought him some tulips last week. Picked them from one of the hospital flowerbeds. I apologized and said I could give them some of our bulbs. He said not at all, it was a sign she was becoming more outgoing. Wanted to know about Ralph and Margaret. I said, 'In what way?' He said, 'No particular way. When she was little.' I said, 'Ralph was fond of her: she was his little girl.' He said, 'Yes.'

Took the dogs up the hill later on.

She picks up the tea chest

They're next I suppose.

She moves to the exit UL

Bloody psychiatrist.

She exits

Music. The Lights fade to Black-out. A moment. The music fades and the Lights come up again

Muriel enters L, *wearing her outdoor coat*

Crack of dawn this morning I routed out my trusty green cossy and spent a happy half-hour breasting the billows. The old cossy's seen better days and the moth had got into the bust but as the only people were one or two brave souls walking the dog I didn't frighten the troops.

Came back hungry as a hunter so boiled myself an egg on the ring and had it with a slice of Ryvita, sitting in the window. Sun just catches it for an hour then, lovely. I tidied the room, did one or two jobs, and then toddled along to the library and had a walk round Boots by which time it was getting on for lunchtime, it's surprising how time does go. When I think of the things I used to get through in the old days I wonder how I did it.

She sits in the armchair, hunched up a little. One should feel it is chilly

Been here about a month now. Got on to it via an advert in *The Lady*. Sledmere it's called, 'Holiday flatlets'. Off season, of course, and quite reasonable. I haven't quite got the town sorted out yet. I feel sure there must be a community here if only I can put my finger on it. I had a word with a young woman at the Town Hall. Blue fingernails but civil enough otherwise. Said was I interested in Meals on Wheels. I said, 'Rather. I was 2 i/c Meals on Wheels for the whole of Sudbury,' a fund of experience. Brawn not too good but

brains available to be picked at any time. She looked a bit blank.
Turns out she meant did I want to be on the receiving end. I said, 'Not
on your life,' but message received and understood. The old girl's
past it. Hence the swim, I suppose.

Still, I soldier on and it's not quite orphans of the storm time. I look
round the shops quite a bit and if I'm lucky I run into Angela
Gillespie who's got her mother in a home here and comes over from
time to time. We have coffee and a natter about the old days. Though
I can't do that too often. Morning coffee these days seems to cost a
king's ransom. And with me there doesn't have to be coffee. I can
talk to anybody. The other morning I got chatting to one of these
young men in orange who bang their tambourines in the precinct.
Came up to me rattling his bowl, shaven head but otherwise quite
sensible. His view is that life is some kind of prep. Trial run. Thinks
we're being buffed up for a better role next time. As sensible as
anything else I suppose. I said, 'Well, I just hope it's not in
Hunstanton.' (*She laughs*)

The big bright spot on the horizon is Margaret. Heaps better, lost a
lot of weight, got rid of that terrible cardigan and now is quite a good-
looking young woman. In a hostel up to pres. but planning on getting
a small flat. Came down last week and says next time it could be
under her own steam, takes her driving test in ten days. Miracle. She
took me out to lunch just like a normal girl. Talked about Ralph et
cetera. Doesn't blame him, wishes he were alive. I don't know what
I think. Sorry for him, I suppose. She paid the bill and left a tip, just
as if she'd been doing it all her life. Of course she'll be nicely off
now, Ralph tied it all up so tight even Giles couldn't get his hands
on it, the rascal.

Don't see him and Pippa much, not a peep out of them for over a
month now. Doesn't upset me. Miss the tinies. Not so tiny, Lucy'll
be twelve now. And twelve is like fifteen these days. Married next.
I'd seen myself as a model grandmother, taking them to *Peter Pan*
and the Science Museum. Not to be. Another dream bites the dust.

My big passion now is the telly box. Never bothered with it before. These days I watch it all the time. And I'm not the discerning viewer. No fear. Rubbish. Australian series in the afternoons, everything. Glued to it all. Fan.

The dialogue is more broken up now

I sometimes wonder if I killed Ralph. All those death-dealing breakfasts. We haven't had much weather to speak of. Eat less now. A buttered scone goes a long way.

She picks up a Walkman and headphones

This is my new toy. Seen children with them, never appreciated what they were. Asked a young man for a listen in the precinct. Revelation. Saved up and bought one. Get the cassettes out of the library. Worth its weight in gold. Marvellous.

She puts it on and henceforth speaks in bursts and too loudly. During the following, she takes some gloves out of her pocket and puts them on

I wouldn't want you to think this was a tragic story.

Pause

I'm not a tragic woman.

Pause

I'm not that type.

The Lights fade

CURTAIN

FURNITURE AND PROPERTY LIST

On stage: Upright upholstered chair
                 Upright chair
                 Side table

Off stage: Envelopes
                 Tea chest
                 Walkman and headphones

LIGHTING PLOT

Practical fittings required: nil
Interior. The same scene throughout

To open: General interior lighting

Cue 1	**Muriel** exits *Fade lights*	(Page 3)
Cue 2	**Muriel** sits in the armchair *Bring up lights*	(Page 3)
Cue 3	**Muriel**: "One keeps forgetting that." *Fade lights*	(Page 6)
Cue 4	**Muriel** sits in the armchair *Bring up lights*	(Page 6)
Cue 5	**Muriel**: " ... I never heard Ralph mention it." *Fade lights*	(Page 9)
Cue 6	**Muriel** stands behind the armchair *Bring up lights*	(Page 9)
Cue 7	**Muriel** exits *Fade lights*	(Page 11)
Cue 8	When ready *Bring up lights*	(Page 11)
Cue 9	**Muriel**: "I'm not that type." *Fade lights*	(Page 13)

EFFECTS PLOT

Cue 1   **Muriel** exits   (Page 3)
          Music

Cue 2   **Muriel** sits in the armchair   (Page 3)
          Fade music

Cue 3   **Muriel**: "One keeps forgetting that."   (Page 6)
          Music

Cue 4   **Muriel** sits in the armchair   (Page 6)
          Fade music

Cue 5   **Muriel**: " ... I never heard Ralph mention it."   (Page 9)
          Music

Cue 6   **Muriel** stands behind the armchair   (Page 9)
          Fade music

Cue 7   **Muriel** exits   (Page 11)
          Music

Cue 8   When ready   (Page 11)
          Fade music